Dear Little One,

Who made you? That's right. God made you.
God loves you and would like you to love Him and
His Son, Jesus.
We hope you will enjoy this Bible and that it will be
a reminder of how important God and Jesus can be in
your life.
It is full of wonderful stories and adventures and
teaches us all how God watches over and cares for us.

Happy Reading,   *Robert Hick*

Presented to

....

By

....

On

....

BEDTIME
Bible Stories
for Children

ADAPTED FROM THE OLD
AND NEW TESTAMENTS

Two hundred beautiful
colour pictures by
Diane Matthews.

Bible stories from the Old
and New Testaments
selected by Georgette
Butcher.

The Bible

Stories from The
Old Testament

Contents

Many of the stories in this book.

Noah builds the ark

Joseph's coat of many colours

Baby Moses is found in the rushes

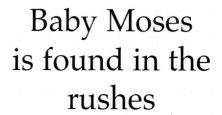

The burning bush

A path through the Red Sea

God's ten good laws

Ruth
goes to
serve God

God
calls
Samuel

David
and
Goliath

Queen Esther helps the Jews

Daniel in the lion pit

Jonah and the big fish

In the beginning God made the world. It was very beautiful. God made the birds to fly in the sky, fish to swim in the sea, animals to walk on the land and trees and flowers to come from the earth.

God made Adam and Eve, the first man and woman. He gave them a lovely garden to live in. They were happy looking after it. Then they did what God told them not to do. Sadly it meant they had to leave the garden.

Adam and Eve had children and they had children. God was not happy. He told Noah that he would send a flood. Noah was to build a big boat and save his family and some of the animals.

In time there were more people. They spoke the same language. They wanted to be important so they built a big tower. God wasn't pleased and he sent the people away in groups, each with their own language.

Abraham lived in a big town. God and he were very special friends. So when God told him to leave his home Abraham obeyed. He took his animals and his family and they slept in tents as they made the long journey.

Abraham's wife Sarah was sad because they did not have a baby. God had promised them that they would have a son.
God did keep his promise because after a long time Isaac was born.

When Isaac was grown up, his father, Abraham asked his best friend to find a wife for Isaac. God led him to Rebecca as she was fetching water at the well. When Isaac and Rebecca met they loved each other.

or a long time Isaac and Rebecca did not have children. So Isaac prayed to God and God gave them twin boys. Esau was a hunter but Jacob stayed near the home.

ne day, when Jacob
had cooked some
stew, Esau came in
very hungry. He asked for
food. 'Only if you give me
your right to be head of the
family,' said Jacob. And Esau
was so hungry he agreed.

Isaac became old and blind. He wanted to bless his eldest son, Esau. Jacob's mother dressed him to be like Esau and so Isaac blessed him instead. Esau had lost his blessing. Jacob's family later grew and became the nation of Israel.

Esau was angry with Jacob. So Jacob was sent to his Uncle Laban. He helped Rachel, a shepherd girl, water her sheep. She was Laban's daughter. Laban agreed that Jacob should work seven years and then marry Rachel.

Jacob loved his son Joseph. He made him a lovely coat. It made his brothers hate him. Joseph had a dream in which his family was bowing to him. His brothers laughed at it and were unkind to him.

One day they put Joseph down a dry well. They hoped he would die. Then one of his brothers thought it better to sell him to some men passing by. So Joseph was taken to Egypt. There he was sold as a slave.

Joseph was sold to the captain of the king's guard. The king had a dream. God helped Joseph to tell him what it meant. The king was pleased.
He put him in charge of food in the country.

Jacob needed corn. He sent his sons to Egypt to buy some. Joseph knew his brothers. He forgave them for selling him. Later, Jacob and all the family came to live in Egypt.

The king of Egypt did not want little Hebrew boys to live. When Moses was born, his mother hid him in a basket at the edge of the river. The king's daughter found him. She looked after him and brought him up.

When Moses was grown up he left Egypt. One day on the mountain he saw a bush on fire. He went to look and heard God speaking to him. 'I am sending you to Egypt to lead my people out.' Moses was afraid but trusted God and obeyed.

he King of Egypt
did not want the
Israelites to go.
They worked very hard for
him. So God made a lot of
nasty things happen. He
sent plagues of frogs,
gnats and flies. At last the
king said, 'Get out, leave
my country.'

The children of Israel were in the desert for forty years. God led them by a cloud by day and a pillar of fire by night. He also fed them day by day.

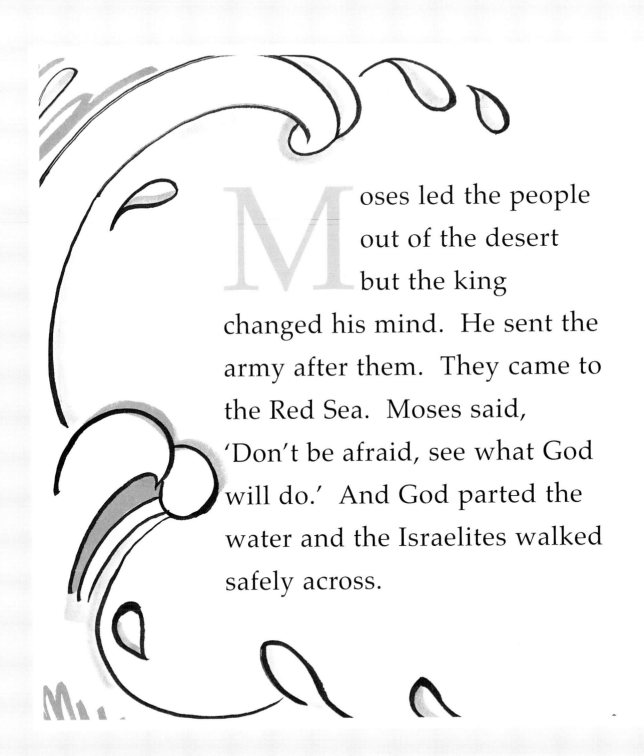

Moses led the people out of the desert but the king changed his mind. He sent the army after them. They came to the Red Sea. Moses said, 'Don't be afraid, see what God will do.' And God parted the water and the Israelites walked safely across.

God wrote ten laws on slabs of stone. He gave them to Moses. He said that all his people must obey them. It would help them every day.

oses went apart to speak with God. The Israelites made a golden calf. They called it their god. God was angry. Moses prayed to God for them. God heard. He punished them but he forgave them.

oses wanted so much to see God. So what God did was to place Moses alone in a cave. In the cave, Moses became aware of God's presence and was happy.

God asked for gifts. He wanted a tent made. It was very beautiful. Then the clouds covered it. Inside was a bright light, showing God was there. He wanted to show he was with his people.

The people of Israel grumbled. God was not pleased. He sent snakes to bite them. The people were sorry. God told Moses to make a snake of copper. If the people looked up to it they would recover from the snake bites.

alaam was not a nice man. He wanted to upset God's people. God stopped him by stopping the donkey. Balaam beat the donkey. God told Balaam he was wrong to go on the journey. Balaam was sorry and he obeyed God.

oses climbed to the top of a mountain. God showed him all the promised land. He would give it to the Jews. But Moses would not go in. Moses died and God buried him. No one knows where God buried Moses.

Ruth's husband died. She went to his country. She wanted to serve his God. Ruth worked in the harvest fields. She met Boaz there and soon they married. David, Israel's great king, was her great-grandson.

Hannah was sad. She did not have a baby. It made her cry very much. So she prayed to God. God heard and gave her a baby boy. Hannah thanked God and said that Samuel should serve him.

amuel lived at the temple. One night he heard God calling him. God told Samuel about things he was going to do. Samuel grew up listening and talking to God.

God sent Samuel to choose a king. Jesse's sons were big and strong. 'No' said Samuel. 'Not these. Have you another son?' David was in the field. When he came, God said, 'This is the one.' Samuel anointed him as king.

avid was chosen
by God to be king
after Saul. Saul
did not know this. When
Saul was unhappy David
would play his harp. This
made Saul feel better.

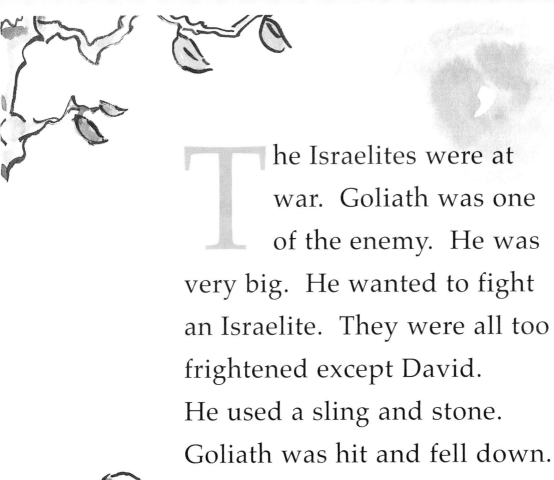

The Israelites were at war. Goliath was one of the enemy. He was very big. He wanted to fight an Israelite. They were all too frightened except David. He used a sling and stone. Goliath was hit and fell down.

David wrote songs. One was about God as a shepherd. We are like his sheep. The shepherd finds food for the sheep. He looks after them. He is always with them. He takes away their fear.

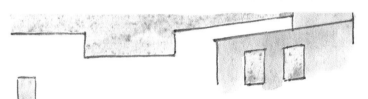

Another song tells us to sing to God. We should praise him. He made us. We belong to him. We should thank him and praise him. He is good and will always love us.

olomon was the son of
King David. He was a
good man. God asked
him, 'What would you like
me to give you?'
Solomon asked to be wise.
This would help him to look
after his people.

The Queen of Sheba heard that Solomon was wise and rich. She came to see him and liked what she saw. 'Praise the Lord your God,' she said. She knew that God had made him wise to rule over the people.

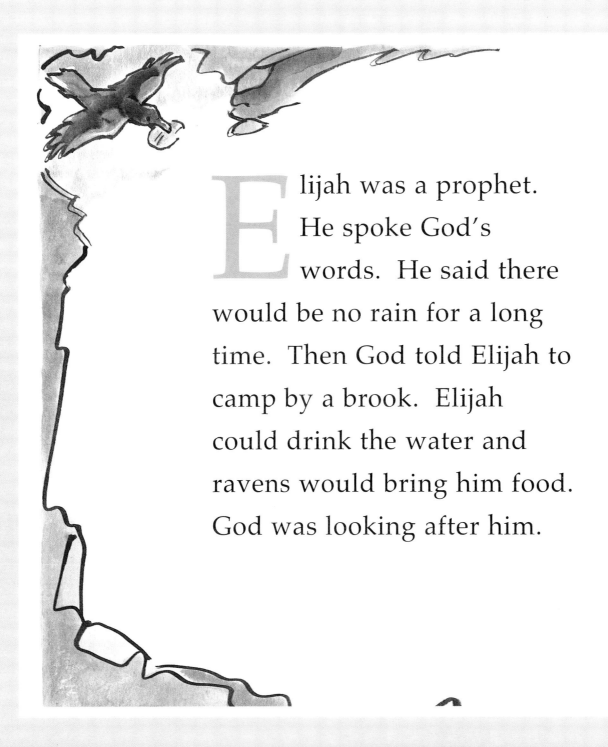

Elijah was a prophet. He spoke God's words. He said there would be no rain for a long time. Then God told Elijah to camp by a brook. Elijah could drink the water and ravens would bring him food. God was looking after him.

lisha wanted to be like
Elijah. God was going
to take Elijah to
heaven. If Elisha saw him
go, said Elijah, his wish
would be granted. He saw a
chariot and horses of fire take
Elijah. His coat fell and
Elisha picked it up and it
became his. He now knew
his wish had been granted.

Naaman was a great soldier. He was very sick. The king sent God's prophet, Elisha. Elisha said Naaman was to wash in the River Jordan. Naaman did so and was cured. He thanked God.

Josiah became king. He rebuilt the temple. A workman found the book of the Law. God had given the Law to Moses. When Josiah heard the Law he tore his clothes. He was sad because the people had forgotten God.

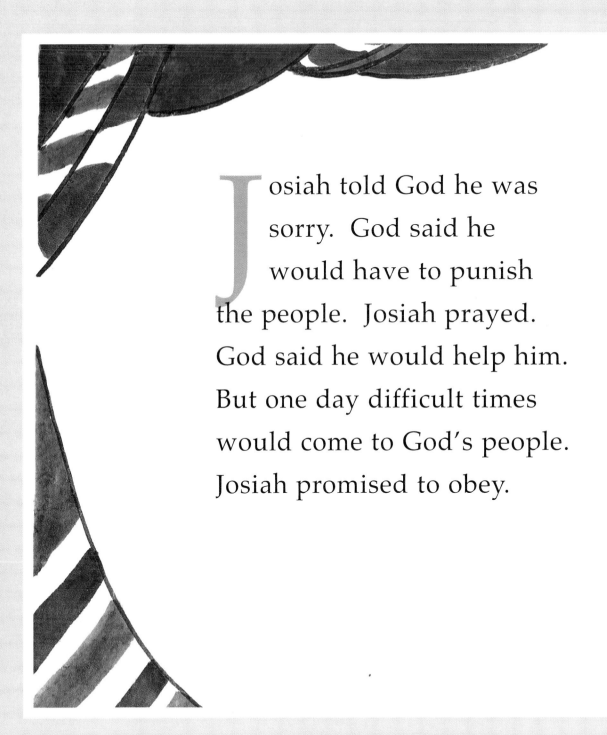

Josiah told God he was sorry. God said he would have to punish the people. Josiah prayed. God said he would help him. But one day difficult times would come to God's people. Josiah promised to obey.

Nehemiah served a king. Nehemiah was sad because his home town was in ruins. He prayed that the king would let him go back. His prayer was answered. He spent many years building and helping the people. All the time he prayed for God's help.

Esther was a queen. When the Jews were in trouble she knew God wanted her to help. She went to the king's palace. The king held out the gold sceptre to allow her in. She told how the Jews were being harmed and the king helped them.

A wonderful day will come, said Isaiah. God had told him that wild animals will live peacefully together. Children will take care of them. They will be safe. They will play with the animals.

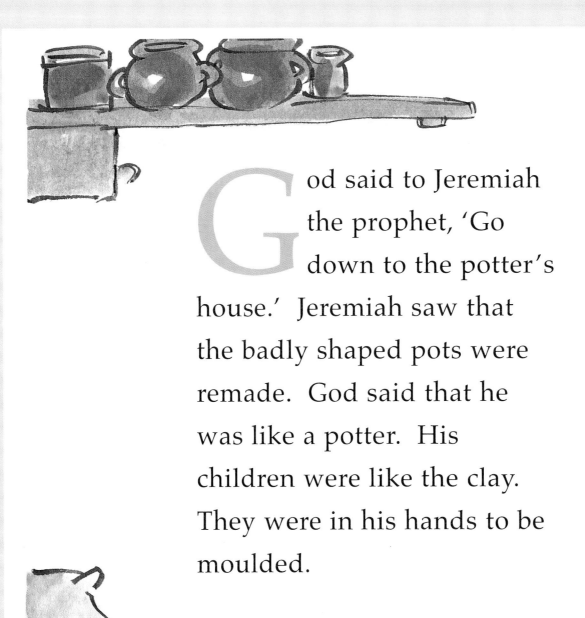

God said to Jeremiah the prophet, 'Go down to the potter's house.' Jeremiah saw that the badly shaped pots were remade. God said that he was like a potter. His children were like the clay. They were in his hands to be moulded.

Jeremiah was put down a dry well. His friend, Ebedmelech went to save Jeremiah. He sent down old clothes to put under his arms. Jeremiah was safely pulled up.

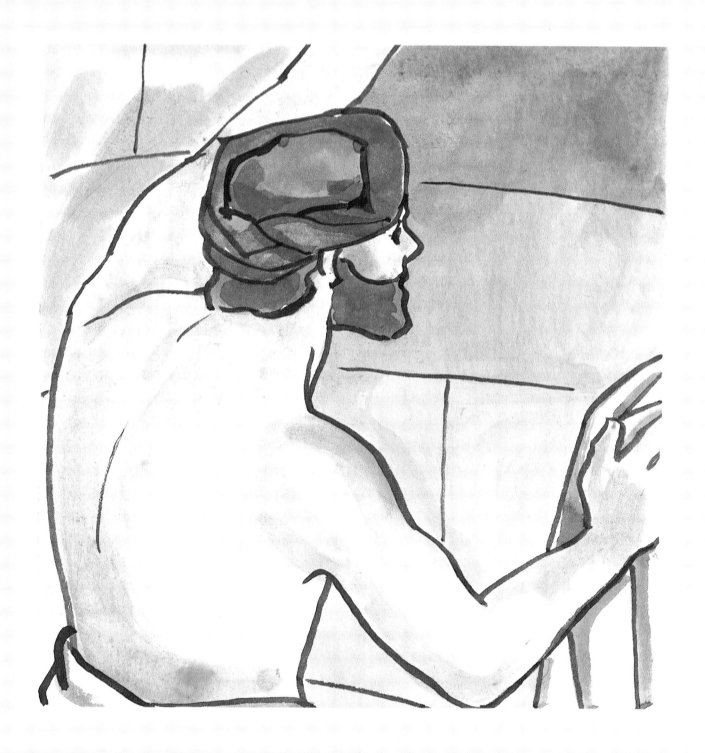

aniel and his friends were taken to a strange country. The people there did not know God. Because Daniel prayed he was punished. He was thrown into a pit with lions. But God kept Daniel quite safe.

The king gave a great feast. Suddenly, a hand was seen writing on the wall. No one except Daniel could say what it meant. The king did not love god, said Daniel. He would no longer be king.

113

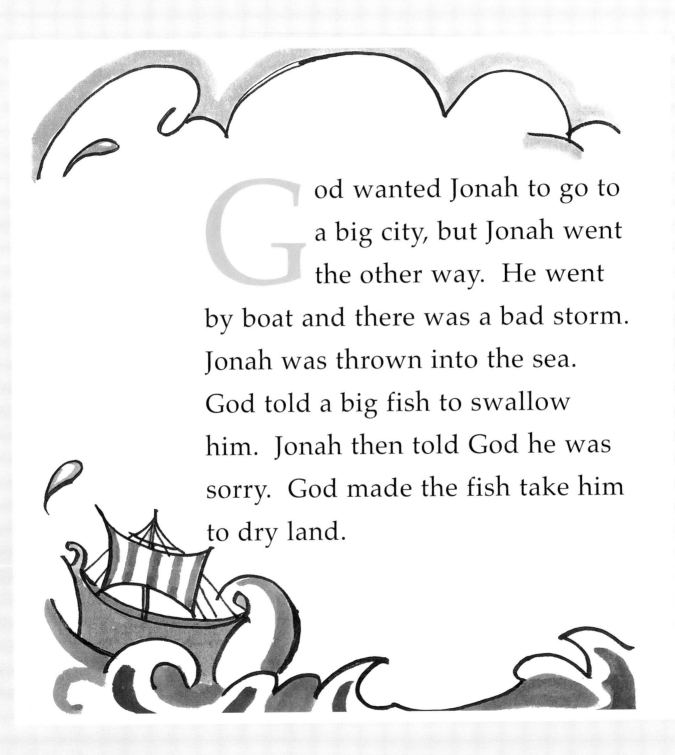

God wanted Jonah to go to a big city, but Jonah went the other way. He went by boat and there was a bad storm. Jonah was thrown into the sea. God told a big fish to swallow him. Jonah then told God he was sorry. God made the fish take him to dry land.

Do you know?

Who made you?

Do you know?

Who were the first people on
the earth?

Do you know?

Who built the ark?

Do you know?

Who had a coat of many
colours?

Answer: Joseph

Do you know?

Who was the baby found in the rushes?

Answer: Moses

Do you know?

What happened when Moses
and his people reached the
Red Sea?

Do you know?

How many laws God told
Moses to write?

Answer: Ten good laws.

Do you know?

Who was it that
David fought?

Answer: Goliath

Do you know?

Who was thrown into a pit
with lions?

Do you know?

Who was swallowed by
a big fish?

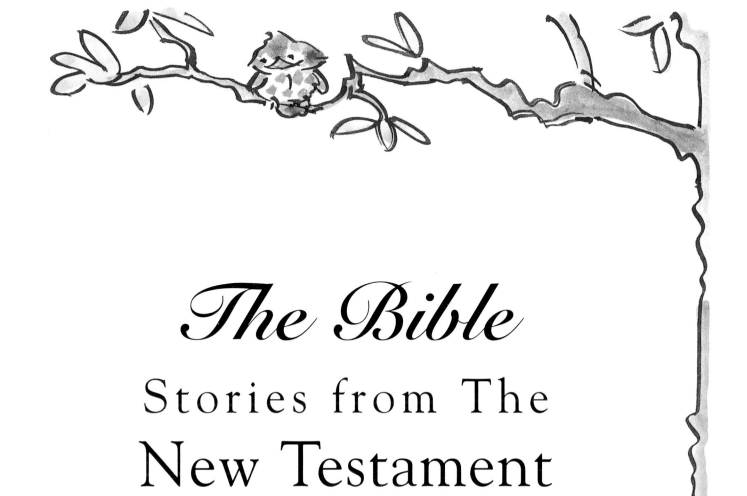

The Bible

Stories from The
New Testament

Contents

Many of the stories in this book.

Jesus gets the dinner

The rich poor woman

Jesus saves a little sick girl

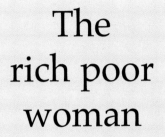

The good samaritan

A man comes through the roof

The boy who left home

The last supper

Judas betrays his friend

The cock crows twice

A very sad day

Where has Jesus Gone?

Heaven - what will it be like?

God's angel came to Mary. He told her she was to have a baby. He would be called Jesus and would be God's son. Mary was surprised but told God she only wanted to obey him.

When Jesus was born shepherds were in the fields. An angel came and told them. He said Jesus would do wonderful things. The shepherds went to see the baby. They were very happy and praised God.

ise men who
studied the
stars came to
see Jesus. They had been
led by a star from the east.
They wanted to see the
baby who was to be king of
the Jews and brought
presents of gold, incense
and myrrh.

King Herod heard about the baby. He wanted to harm him. God had a plan. He told Joseph in a dream to take Mary and Jesus to Egypt. They left at night and stayed in Egypt until Herod died.

Mary and Joseph took Jesus to the Temple. They met Simeon and Anna who both loved God. When they saw Jesus they were glad and praised God. They knew Jesus was very special.

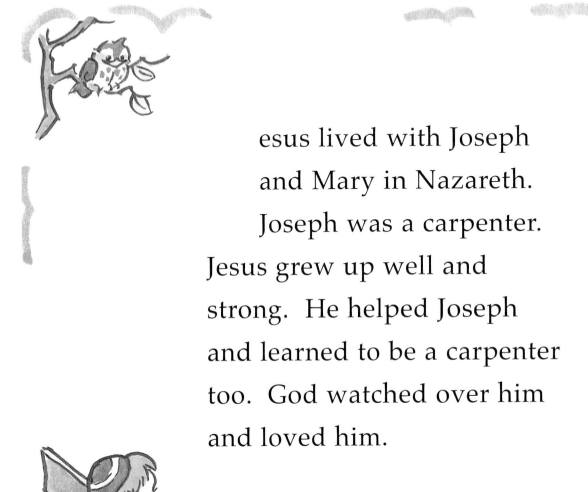

esus lived with Joseph
and Mary in Nazareth.
Joseph was a carpenter.
Jesus grew up well and
strong. He helped Joseph
and learned to be a carpenter
too. God watched over him
and loved him.

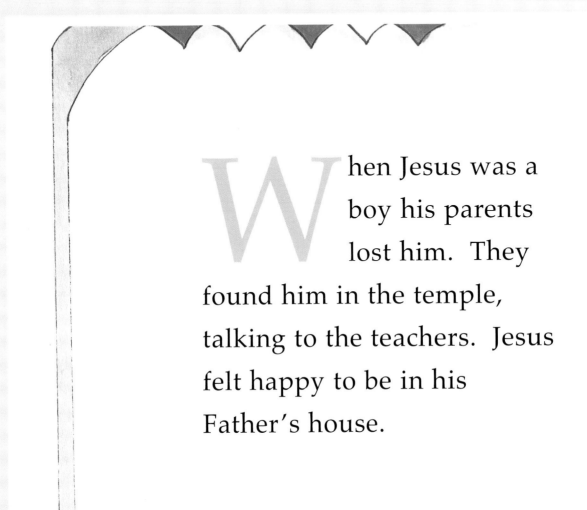

When Jesus was a boy his parents lost him. They found him in the temple, talking to the teachers. Jesus felt happy to be in his Father's house.

ohn gave people a special washing in the river. They came because they were sorry for things they had done. Jesus came, although he was good. When he was in the water, there was a lovely light. God was showing he was pleased with Jesus, his son.

Jesus was walking by the lake. He saw two fishermen catching fish. Jesus said, 'Come with me and I will teach you to catch men.' Simon and his brother Andrew left their nets and followed Jesus.

Jesus was in a boat with his friends. He went to sleep.
A strong wind began to blow.
His friends were frightened.
They quickly woke Jesus.
Jesus told the wind to stop.
All was calm.

Jesus was talking to a large crowd about God. It began to get dark. The people were hungry. His friends wondered how to feed them. They had five loaves and two fish. Jesus thanked God and there was enough to feed them all.

ome people brought
a man to Jesus. He
could not hear or
speak very well. Jesus
touched his ears and his
tongue. 'Open up,' he
said. And the man was
able to hear and to speak.

Jesus and his friends went to see Martha and Mary. Mary listened to all Jesus said. Martha was cross because she was doing all the work.
But Jesus said Mary was right to take the time to learn from him.

here was a very rich man. He was happy to have so much. But God said to him, 'Tonight you will give up your life and leave all that you have behind you.' Just having things does not make us rich in God's eyes. God has given us a wonderful world.

God, said Jesus, made the birds and flowers. He feeds the birds. He gave flowers pretty colours. He made the grass green. They don't worry. Nor should we. God loves us. He will feed and dress us, said Jesus.

A woman had ten silver coins. But she lost one. She looked hard for it. When she found it she was happy. She told everyone. All heaven is glad when we come to love Jesus.

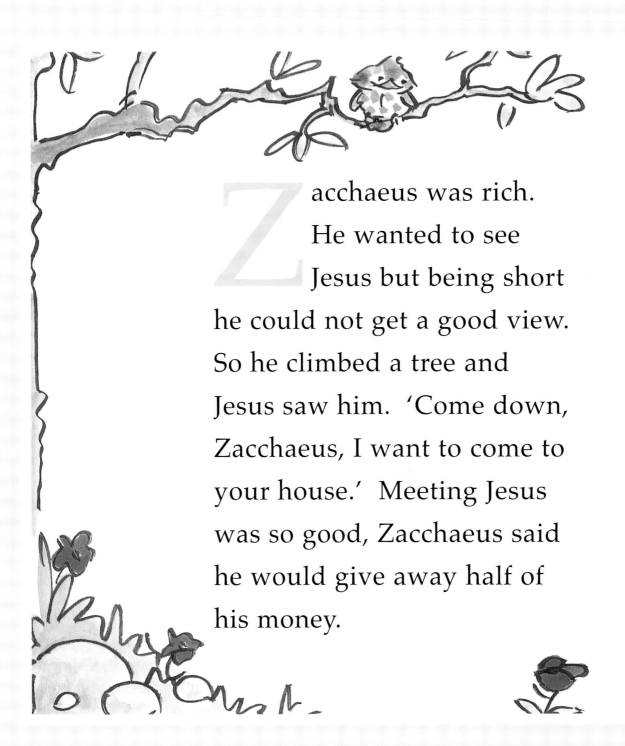

Zacchaeus was rich.
He wanted to see
Jesus but being short
he could not get a good view.
So he climbed a tree and
Jesus saw him. 'Come down,
Zacchaeus, I want to come to
your house.' Meeting Jesus
was so good, Zacchaeus said
he would give away half of
his money.

It is good to obey Jesus, like the man who built his house on a rock. When the winds came the house stood strong. Another man built his house on sand. When the rains came his house fell down with a crash.

Rich men were giving money in the Temple. Jesus was watching them. He saw a poor woman. She put in two small coins. Jesus said, 'She has put in more than the others. She has given all she has.'

eople brought
children to Jesus,
but his friends
wanted them to go
away. 'Let the children
come to me,' said Jesus.
He took them in his
arms and loved them.

Jairus' little daughter was sick. He asked Jesus to help. At the house everyone was crying. They said, 'She is dead.' Jesus said, 'Don't cry.' Then he took the girl's hand. 'Get up, my child.' She stood up, well and happy.

esus wants us to love each other. He told a story. A man was robbed and hurt. Another man, passing by, saw him and went on. A second did the same. A third man stopped. He bandaged him and took him to an inn to rest. He was kind.

Jesus was in a house. He was talking to a crowd of people. Suddenly, a bed came through the roof. Four men had brought their friend to Jesus. He was sick. Jesus forgave him and healed him.

Jesus told a story. A man asked his father for money. He went away. He quickly spent the money on silly things. He found work looking after pigs. He was so hungry he wanted to eat the pig's food. No one gave him any food.

he son who ran away
thought about home.
There, everyone had
food. He had been wrong.
He would go home and say
sorry. His father saw him
coming. He was so glad to
see him he gave a big party.

ne evening Jesus
poured water into a
bowl. He began to
wash his friends' feet. 'No!'
said Peter, 'not mine.'
'Unless I wash your feet,'
said Jesus, 'we cannot be
friends.' 'Then wash all of
me,' Peter said.

Jesus rode on a donkey into Jerusalem. There was a big crowd of people. They cut branches from the trees. They stood waving to him as Jesus rode along. They praised him as God's son.

Jesus had a meal with his twelve friends. It was special. But he knew one of them would hurt him. They wanted to know who would do such a thing. Jesus gave a piece of bread to Judas. He was the one.

Jesus was talking to God, his Father, in a garden. A large crowd came looking for him. Judas came up and kissed him. It was to let the people know this was Jesus. The men took Jesus away.

Peter said he would never disown Jesus. 'Before the cock crows twice you will,' said Jesus. Jesus was on trial. Peter waited outside. Three times he told people he was not a friend. Then the cock crowed a second time.

Jesus was hurt by cruel men. The soldiers put a crown of thorns on his head. They made him carry a heavy cross. The crowds watched him. He walked to the place where he was to die.

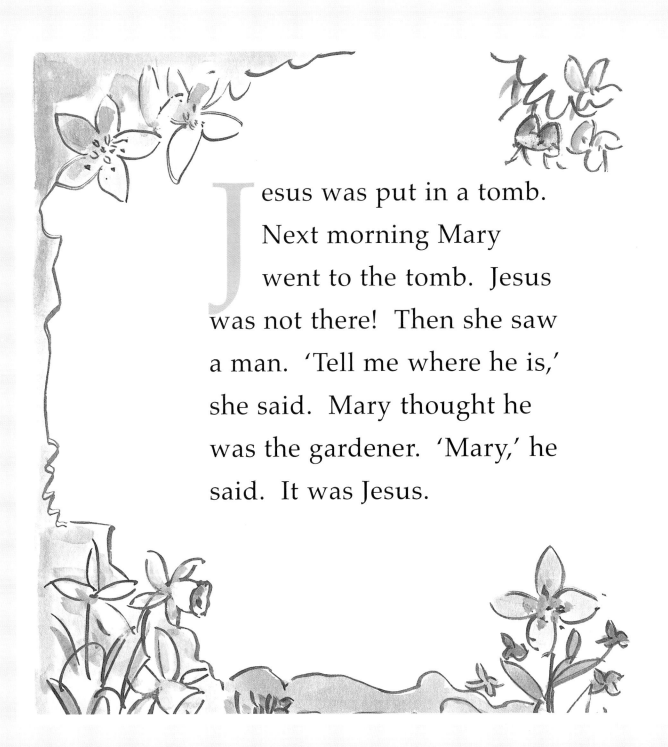

Jesus was put in a tomb. Next morning Mary went to the tomb. Jesus was not there! Then she saw a man. 'Tell me where he is,' she said. Mary thought he was the gardener. 'Mary,' he said. It was Jesus.

The time came for Jesus to leave. He was going to God, his Father. His friends watched as he went up into the sky. A cloud hid him and he was gone.

any who loved
Jesus were in
one room.
Suddenly, there was the
noise of the wind. What
looked like little flames
touched everyone. It was a
sign of the Holy Spirit. He
had come to be with them.

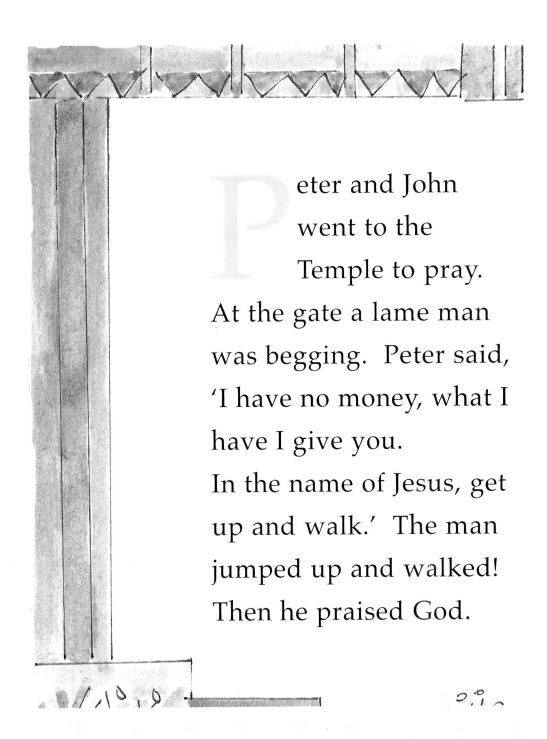

Peter and John went to the Temple to pray. At the gate a lame man was begging. Peter said, 'I have no money, what I have I give you.
In the name of Jesus, get up and walk.' The man jumped up and walked! Then he praised God.

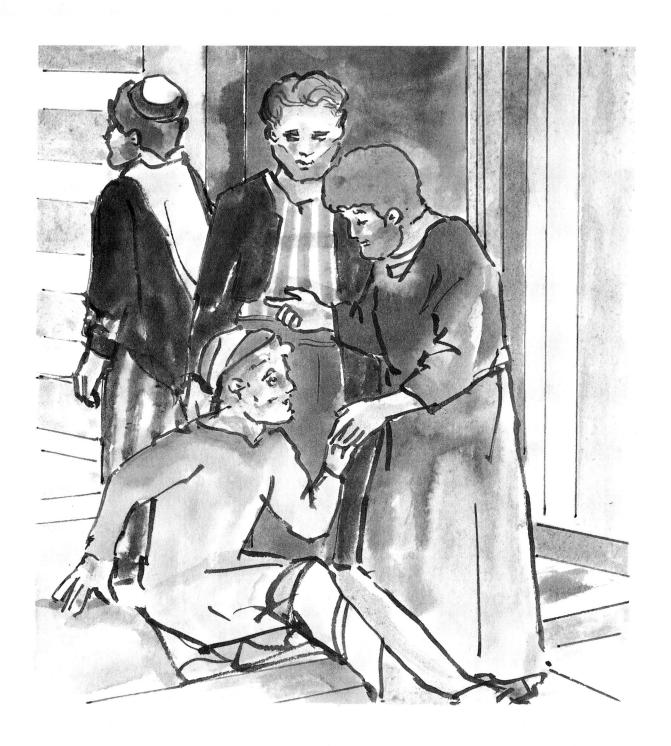

tephen, a brave man, did great things for God. Some people were against him. Stephen spoke about Jesus. His face glowed with love. The men were angry. They threw stones at Stephen until he died and went to be with Jesus.

Saul hated the Christians. But one day a bright light shone around him. He heard a voice calling him. He knew that it was Jesus. It made him want to follow Jesus. After that he loved Jesus and worked for him.

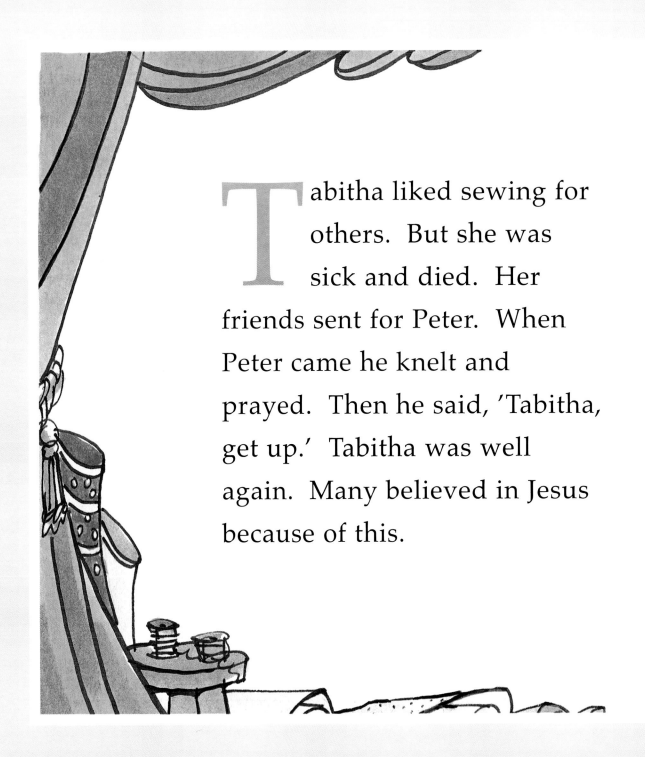

Tabitha liked sewing for others. But she was sick and died. Her friends sent for Peter. When Peter came he knelt and prayed. Then he said, 'Tabitha, get up.' Tabitha was well again. Many believed in Jesus because of this.

Saul changed his name to Paul. He began to talk about Jesus. It made some people cross. They wanted to harm him. His friends helped him to get away. They lowered him in a basket over the town wall.

eter talked about Jesus. So he was put in prison. His friends were praying hard that he might be freed. Peter was asleep. An angel came and woke him and told Peter to follow him out of prison.

Peter had escaped from prison knowing God had helped him. He went and knocked at the house where his friends were. The girl who came was so glad it was Peter, at first she forgot to open the door!

aul met some women praying by the river. One of them, Lydia, believed Paul when he said how much Jesus loved her. She invited Paul and his friends to stay at her house. Those who loved Jesus began to meet there.

Paul and Silas were put into prison. As they prayed, there was an earthquake. All the doors opened. The jailer thought the prisoners had gone. Paul called to tell him they were safe.

The jailer said, 'What must I do to be saved?' 'Believe,' said Paul. He and Silas told him all about Jesus. The jailer and his family wanted to love Jesus. That night they became Christians.

Paul was on a ship.
He was going to Rome.
There was a big storm. An
angel told Paul not to be afraid.
They would be saved. They had to
swim ashore but they were safe.

Timothy had a mother and grandmother who loved God. They taught Timothy from the Bible to love God, which he did when he grew up.

Paul became a prisoner. He still told people about Jesus. He wrote letters to Timothy and other friends. He wanted to help them to love Jesus and learn more about him.

Paul, in one of his letters, wrote about love. Love is kind. Love is not making anyone sad. Love is not rude. Love is not being nasty. We all need to love others. Love is being like Jesus.

ne of Jesus' last
messages was to tell
us that he wants to
come and live with us. He
knocks at the door. He wants
us to invite him in.
He wants always to be a part
of our life.

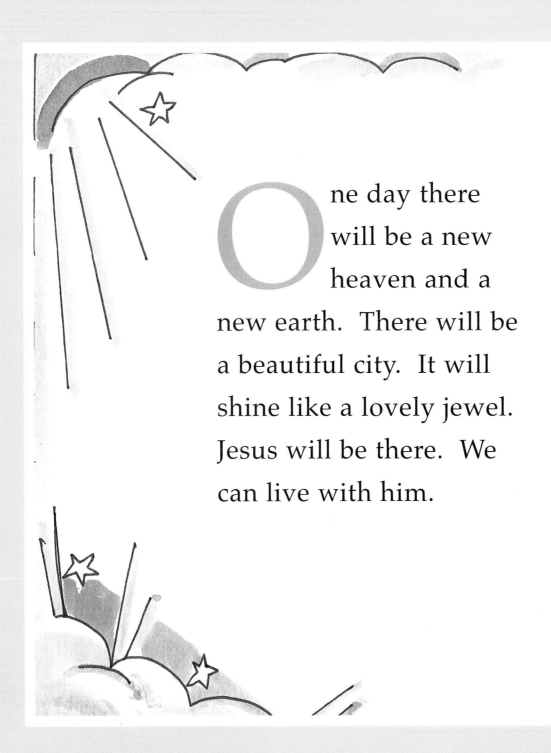

One day there will be a new heaven and a new earth. There will be a beautiful city. It will shine like a lovely jewel. Jesus will be there. We can live with him.

Do you know?

Who was Jesus' mother?

Do you know?

What presents did the three
wise men bring?

Do you know?

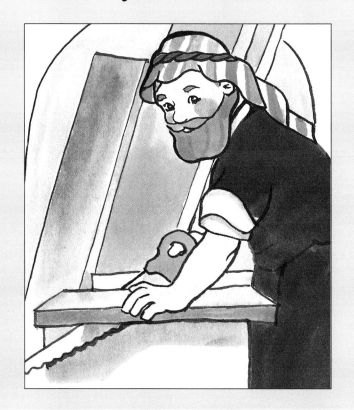

What job did Joseph have?

Do you know?

Who gave Jesus a special
washing in the river?

Do you know?

Who were the fishermen who followed Jesus?

Do you know?

Whose little girl was sick and
saved by Jesus?

Do you know?

Who betrayed Jesus in the
garden by kissing him?

Do you know?

What did the soldiers make
Jesus carry to the place
where he was to die?

Answer: A heavy cross.

Do you know?

Who did Mary think Jesus was when she went to the tomb?

Answer: The gardener.

Do you know?

Where did Jesus go when it
was time to leave?

A CHILD'S BOOK OF PRAYERS

PRAYERS ABOUT FEELINGS. Sometimes we feel happy because we had a good time. Then it's good to say thank you to God. At other times we may feel lonely, angry or sorry. God wants us to tell him about those feelings, too.

I smile when I am happy.
I scream when I am scared.
I frown when I am jealous.
I cry when I am sad.
Thank you God for all these
feelings, good or bad.

I will praise you, O Lord with all my heart;
I will tell of all your wonders
I will be glad and rejoice in you;
I will sing praise to your name
O Most High.
AMEN.
Psalm 9:1-2 NIV

And a little child
shall lead them.'
ISAIAH 7

When I was a child, I spoke
as a child, I understood as a child,
I thought as a child.
1 CORINTHIANS 13

Dear God, We had the "giggles" today! There were so many funny things to laugh at with each other. And we were doing lots of silly things such as funny faces, silly rhymes, and jumping on the beds. Thank you for a fun time! Love from me. AMEN.

Dear God, When I'm quiet I sit by myself and think about how you are all about me. And that makes me feel happy.
AMEN.

Dear Jesus, Please help me not to feel cross because it makes me feel bad.
AMEN.

Dear God,
You made the thunder.
It's just like when I'm angry.
You made things just like our feelings.
So you know how I feel.
Help me not to be angry.
AMEN.

D ear Jesus,

I don't think anybody loves me today.

Everybody's grumpy and cross.

But you're not.

You love me like I'm special. Always.

I'm glad I'm your friend today.

AMEN.

ear Jesus,

I want someone to play with.

But everyone else already has
someone to play with. Except me.
I feel sad and lonely.
Help me to remember just how
much you love me Jesus because
that makes me feel better, like I'm
not quite alone.
Because I know you
are my friend.
AMEN.

Finally, whatsoever things are true
Whatsoever things are honest
Whatsoever things are just
Whatsoever things are pure
Whatsoever things are lovely
Whatsoever things are of good report
If there be any virtue and if there be any praise
Think on these things.

PAUL, 1ST CENTURY LETTER TO PHILIPPIANS

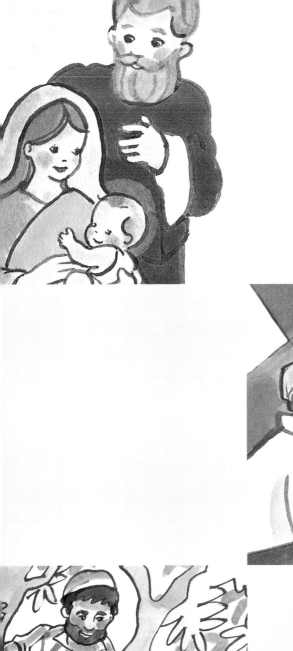